Introducing
Numbers

Introducing
Numbers

A Book for Today

Adrian Reynolds

PTRESOURCES

CHRISTIAN
FOCUS

Copyright © Adrian Reynolds 2013

ISBN 978-1-78191-158-7

First published in 2013 as the introduction to
Teaching Numbers (ISBN 978-1-84550-156-3)
Published as a stand-alone title
in 2013
by
Christian Focus Publications,
Geanies House, Fearn,
Ross-shire, IV20 1TW, Scotland.
with
Proclamation Trust Resources,
Willcox House, 140-148 Borough High Street,
London, SE1 1LB, England, Great Britain.
www.proctrust.org.uk

www.christianfocus.com

Cover design by Daniel van Straaten
Printed by Bell and Bain

CONTENTS

Editor's Preface

Numbers must be one of the least-read Bible books. I think that's a great shame. As someone who has had the privilege of preaching through it on two separate occasions as well as teaching it in conferences and our PT Cornhill Training Course, I want everyone to read it! But I realize that there are obstacles to doing so.

The aim of this little series is to help overcome some of those obstacles so that every Christian can be a student of God's Word, listening attentively to what is God saying today. And as you read through this little introduction – and more importantly, as you read through Numbers – I hope you will discover that Numbers really is a book for today.

For sure, it will present you with some challenges. But I urge you to stick with it, reading carefully and prayerfully. For here you will find a very clear encouragement to keep going on your journey to the promised land that awaits every believer in the Lord Jesus Christ.

Originally, these two chapters started life as part of my contribution to our *Teaching...* series. This series is written especially *for* Bible preachers and teachers *by* Bible preachers and teachers. They are more detailed than a devotional book, though not a full commentary; each volume is written to encourage those who have the serious responsibility of teaching God's Word in any context, especially through preaching. Each, therefore, contains analysis of what the passage means, matched together with how it may be taught and applied.

In this edited excerpt, I hope to help ordinary readers (that's all of us!) get to grips with the book. Firstly, I do that by giving some idea of what Numbers is about. What is its theme and why is it so difficult for some people to read? In the second section, I'll show you why Numbers is an important book today and well worth your time. I'll take you to some other Bible passages that explain the place of Numbers in the overall Bible story. Finally, I'll try to give some practical tips for reading this particular Bible book.

I have edited these two chapters to provide you with a general introduction to the book. Like a traveller who steps off a plane or train at an unfamiliar destination and needs a moment to gather his or her bearings, this short book is designed to help you get your bearings in the book of Numbers.

In reading it, I sincerely hope and pray that your enthusiasm for Numbers will be kindled and that you will come to see that Numbers is not just an obscure Old Testament travelogue. It is a glorious part of Scripture that both shows us Christ and encourages us to live for Him as we journey to the glorious future that awaits us in Him.

Perhaps you have been given this little book as part of a Bible study series or preaching series at church? Then, I hope it both introduces Numbers well and gives you enthusiasm for what lies ahead. Perhaps you have simply picked it up and thought, 'Yes, I'd like to know a bit more about Numbers'? I trust your prayer will be answered. If you enjoy it, as I trust you will, why not buy the full volume, *Teaching Numbers*, particularly if you are in any kind of Bible teaching ministry in the church?

About The Proclamation Trust

The Proclamation Trust is a U.K.-based charity that serves churches by championing the cause of expository Bible preaching and teaching. Our aim is to equip and encourage faithful Bible preachers and teachers wherever they may be found, but particularly in the U.K. We do that through our training course (The Cornhill Training Course) and through conferences, online resources and books.

Our *Teaching…* series is a key part of that work and there are currently twelve volumes in the series.

Our conviction is that where the Bible is faithfully and prayerfully taught God's voice is clearly heard. The call of every Bible teacher is therefore to cast himself fully upon God and, in the words of the Apostle Paul to young Pastor Timothy, to 'correctly handle the word of truth' (2 Tim. 2:15). Many resources, including our blog, The Proclaimer, are available from our website, www.proctrust.org.uk, where you can also read more about our work and ministry.

Adrian Reynolds
Series Editor, London, February 2013

I

Finding your way around Numbers

Lots of people get lost in Numbers. They set out, intending to read the book carefully and thoroughly but it ends up defeating them. It hardly seems full of promising material for the man or woman who wants to be a close follower of Jesus Christ. And not only does it seem distant from us in terms of time and geography, but the very nature of the book seems to discourage fruitful study: long lists, lots of numbers (what else?), laws, obscure stories, and, on the whole, a rather downbeat feeling of rebellion after rebellion.

But, as I hope to show, this could hardly be further from the truth: both Old and New Testament writers look back to the book of Numbers as an important part of the believer's instruction; it foreshadows Christ as clearly as perhaps any of the Pentateuch (the first five books of the Bible); and its lessons are still relevant for a wandering generation today as we make our way towards our promised land. It ends on a high note with those we could call the heroines of the book, Zelophehad's five daughters, the women who walked by faith (chs. 27 and 36).

Reading through Numbers and perhaps studying it in a small group should be thus fruitful and rewarding. However, it will not be without certain challenges. There are some long and difficult passages, and Numbers is one of the rare places which some English translations dare to miss out words (some versions do not translate 7:12-83, for example).

As with all Scripture, the Bible-believing Christian must be in no doubt that God's Spirit has inspired material that will teach, rebuke, correct and train in righteousness. But, perhaps uniquely, the challenges of Numbers will mean that the Bible-believing Christian will have to work hard at 'correctly handling the word of truth'.

WHY IS NUMBERS SUCH A HARD BOOK TO UNDERSTAND?

Perhaps a good place to start is to be honest about some of the challenges that a book like Numbers presents? Broadly these fall into five categories.

- **The challenge of unfamiliarity.** Perhaps chief amongst our hurdles is that few people know the book of Numbers well, if at all. A lot of the material is simply unfamiliar.

There's no substitute for reading a book through, but I hope this little introduction will go some way to helping overcome that challenge.

And such a challenge becomes a self-fulfilling prophecy, for we tend to shy away from that which is unfamiliar, only serving to make it more so. I hope that we shall see that unfamiliarity is no cause for overlooking this rich seam of the Old Testament.

- **The challenge of relevance**. Numbers, like many Old Testament books, seems rather distant from twenty-first-century life. This is compounded by the fact that most of the action takes place neither in Egypt (like Exodus) nor in Canaan (like Joshua) nor even on the brink of entry into Canaan (like Deuteronomy). Rather, we find ourselves in a nowhere place called *the wilderness*. The barrenness of such a place can easily correspond to irrelevance. However, we need to be reassured that the Bible's own commentary on Numbers (such as we find in the Psalms, in Paul and in Hebrews) sees the distance as no barrier at all; quite the opposite in fact, drawing parallels with our own spiritual journey.

• **The challenge of genre**. For the reader, Numbers is an enigmatic book. It contains story, law, poetry and prophecy. Perhaps no other Old Testament book contains quite this mix. Just as the reader has got into the Old Testament narrative way of thinking, then along comes a law section to break it up. No sooner have the prophet's words been ringing in our ears than we are brought to earth with a bump as we read a story about Israel's whoring. Unlike a single-genre book, we need to train ourselves to deal with variety of style and writing.

- **The challenge of obscurity**. Trial by ordeal (5:11-22)? The ground opening up (16:31)? Talking donkeys (22:28)? These are hardly everyday occurrences and the apparent obscurity of such passages makes reading, understanding and inwardly digesting all the harder; though, don't lose heart! The Spirit who inspired the words to be written and preserved lives within us. The challenge is not impossible.

- **The challenge of violence**. As with many Old Testament books, Numbers is not afraid of detailing violence. This comes both from the hand of the Almighty Himself in wrath and judgment, and in the form of battle vengeance against Israel's enemies (though the two are not unconnected). Such brutality grates on modern ears, so much so that some want to deny that the God of the Old Testament is the same as the God of the New. We believe no such thing, of course, but the reader needs to be prepared to understand how these apparently merciless passages faithfully present our loving and just God.

Perhaps the best answer to all of these challenges is to ask what the book of Numbers is all about? What is its overriding theme?

THE THEME OF NUMBERS: A WILDERNESS JOURNEY

Thinking carefully about the theme that runs through the book of Numbers is an important step to understanding a book. If we can determine what purpose the book serves, then we shall find understanding it a much more straightforward task. Moreover, we will have a measure against which to set all our reading to ensure we are seeing what the Holy Spirit intended for the book itself.

Numbers has no key verse or passage to illuminate us. Nevertheless, even a very casual reading of the text tells us that this is a book about a journey. It starts in one place and finishes in another and describes the in-between. The first sentence contains, in Hebrew, a construction which is dependent upon something that has gone before. In other words, it picks up where the previous books have left off. The last passage seems rather abrupt and leaves the reader wondering, 'Well, what happens next?' This creates movement.

The setting of this journey is clear. The people of God have left Egypt (or

are in the process of doing so) where they
have been in slavery to Pharaoh, unable to
free themselves until The Lord's mighty
intervention. God has called them out of
this slavery, providing for their rescue and
sending them on their way to the promised land. Numbers foreshadows the occupation of the land, but apart from a fleet-
ing foray, the people never actually enter
in. That is saved for the conquest book of
Joshua. Numbers describes their journey
to Canaan and the troubles along the way.

Dane Ortlund, director of Bible pub-
lishing at Crossway, has helpfully written
out theme sentences for every Old Testament and New Testament book, relating
them all to the key idea of grace which
is ultimately seen in the gospel of Jesus
Christ. His sentence for Numbers is worth
repeating: 'Numbers shows God's grace in
patiently sustaining his grumbling people
in the wilderness and bringing them to

the border of the promised land not because of them but in spite of them.'[1]

Iain Duguid, in his superb commentary on the book of Numbers,[2] insightfully points out that the journey places the book between what he calls 'salvation accomplished' (the Exodus) and 'salvation completed' (conquest). There is a sense in which the people have received the benefits of the salvation the Lord has won for them, but they have yet to enter into all its fullness. Not surprisingly, this resonates with every New Testament believer: 'We live between the work of God in accomplishing our salvation at the cross and the time when that salvation will be brought to its consummation when Christ returns. We too live between the times.'[3]

---

1   The full list of sentences can be accessed at http://bit. ly/9xvOQ9 (accessed 18 January 2012)

2   Iain M. Duguid, *Numbers: God's Presence in the Wilderness* (Wheaton, U.S.A: Crossway Books, 2006)

3   Duguid, p.19

But how does this idea of living between the times relate to the book of Numbers in particular? Perhaps it is worth pausing at this point and considering the titles of the book. Unusually, it has three, and they're all useful.

Numbers

The name most of us will be familiar with is the name represented in each of our English Bibles: Numbers. This name was also in the Greek version of the Old Testament familiar to Jesus and His followers, the Septuagint. It is a straightforward name and entirely appropriate for a book which has many lists and numbers. However, the primary reason for the name is the two censuses which take place in chapters 1 and 26.

Both count the number of fighting men available to Moses as he leads the people of Israel into the promised land. However, each counts a different generation. The first counts the generation who left Egypt, but their rebellion means that they fall in the wilderness. The second counts the next generation who will enter into and conquer Canaan. As we shall see, these two censuses play an important role in the book and so, far from being a title that would appeal only to accountants and actuaries, this common name is entirely appropriate as well as being illuminating.

In the wilderness

The Jewish Scriptures often have different titles for Old Testament Bible books. They can be useful and often help us see the flow and trajectory of a Bible book. They are mostly found in the opening words or sentence of the text. Numbers is no different on that score, though unusually there are two Hebrew titles which are ascribed to it. The first and most common is 'in the desert' (NIV) or 'in the wilderness' (ESV) taken from 1:1 (the third clause in

Hebrew). The wilderness is the Bible's nowhere place. It is not a place in which to live or flourish, simply a place you pass through from one setting to another.

Such a name conveys movement. No one wants to remain in the wilderness. However, it is not only *geographically* exact, but *spiritually* exact too. Because the people of God rebel against their Saviour they remain in this no-man's-land and eventually meet their death there too. This is the title picked up by Stephen in his majestic biblical history in Acts 7 when he describes Moses as being in the 'assembly *in the desert*' (Acts 7:38, my italics).

It's also an appropriate name for our wanderings. Like the people of Israel, the world is not our home. We have been saved but we are longing, with Abraham, for the 'city with foundations, whose architect and builder is God' (Heb. 11:10). Like Stephen, a more modern hero also picks up on this language: perhaps the most famous Christian book ever written begins with John Bunyan's words, 'As I walked through the *wilderness* of this world....' (*Pilgrim's Progress*, my italics).

And God said...
There is another Hebrew title however. It can be variously translated 'And God said' or 'And Yahweh spoke...' It is an earlier title which fell out of use; in common with many Hebrew titles, it simply picks up the first two Hebrew words of the text. The phrase appears at least 45 times throughout the book. Sometimes this gives rhythm, authority and continuity to apparently disparate passages (for example, 5:1-4, 5-10, 11-31; 6:1-21; 6:22-27). At other times it serves as a word of grace which brings the rebellion of the people into sharp focus. God continues to speak throughout the book of Numbers, in itself a remarkable thing, given what He is subjected to by His people.

These three titles together reinforce the theme of the book which can perhaps be summarized thus: *The Lord accompanies His people on their wilderness journey to the promised land.* The key question then becomes, 'will they make it?' The Scottish preacher James Philip says their challenge is like that expressed by Shakespeare:

> There is a tide in the affairs of men,
> Which, taken at the flood, leads on to fortune;
> Omitted, all the voyage of their life
> Is bound in shallows and in miseries.
> On such a full sea are we now afloat,
> And we must take the current when it serves,
> Or lose our ventures.[4]

This is the question that Numbers answers: will the exiles take the current or lose their ventures, in other words, will they make it to the promised land? To answer that we need to look at the structure of the book.

---

4   William Shakespeare, *Julius Caesar*, Act 4, scene iii.

How is Numbers put together?

Traditionally, most commentators have thought that the book of Numbers is arranged geographically. It's true: most of the action takes place in three locations: Sinai (chs. 1–12), Kadesh Barnea (chs. 13–21) and Moab (chs. 22–36). Each of the first two parts also contains a brief, transitory travel section (in the first case, chapters 11 and 12, in the second, chapters 20 and 21).

This type of structure has much to commend it. First of all, it certainly conveys a progression of sorts. The action starts out at point A, travels through B and comes to an end at C. This fits with what we understood to be the journeying theme of the book. Secondly, it seems to fit neatly with chapter 33. This chapter reads like a travelogue written down by Moses at the Lord's direct command (33:2). Though many of the place names are not mentioned elsewhere in Numbers, the three main locations are referenced in verses 15, 36 and 48.

On this basis, the book splits into three roughly equal sections and it is a popular choice with commentators. But it is not the only, nor the best, choice. It does not really serve the reader and help us to understand what the book is about. Nor, as I will show, does it really reflect the tone and nature of the book's message.

Consider the evidence:

- Whilst all three locations in the book are included in the summary chapter 33 (Sinai in verses 15 and 16; Kadesh Barnea in verses 36 and 37; the plains of Moab in verses 48 and 49), they hardly receive the emphasis one would expect if these were the three major divisions of Numbers. Scan through that chapter and see for yourself.

- Moreover, there are simply too many place names in chapter 33 which are missing from the main text of Numbers for chapter 33 to be a summary of the book and therefore link closely with it. By my count, something like 18 of the names are unique to chapter 33.

- If the travelogue of chapter 33 is to be taken as a geographic guide, it must be noted that it nearly all focuses on the middle geographic section. Sinai barely gets a mention and the plains of Moab, where all the action from chapter 22 onwards takes place, only gets a concluding comment (33:48-49). Once again, the descriptions simply do not fit the text if chapter 33 is to be taken as a kind of index.

- Although such a structure captures the idea of a journey, it ignores the narrative progression of the book. There is a downward spiral in the spiritual well-being of the people. Perhaps this can be illustrated figuratively using a graph? The journey is full of ups and downs, but on the whole the trend is downward until the latter third of the book where things improve significantly.

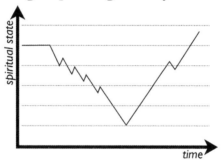

• Plotting the action this way identifies a significant turning point in the narrative where things pick up. This is chapter 26, which happens to be the second census.

A geographical outline takes no account of this division, which is obvious from a careful reading of the text.

There is, however, a different way to read Numbers. It is picked up by some modern commentators and does, I suggest, fit the text and theme very well indeed. According to this analysis, the book of Numbers is essentially the tale of two generations. The first generation leaves Egypt, rebels and perishes in the wilderness. The second generation, born in the wilderness, believes and lives and (eventually in Joshua) gains the promised land. This structure seems to fit all the evidence:

- It does justice to the significance of the two censuses which otherwise become simple counting exercises. On this basis, however, they mark the beginning of the story of each generation. Chapter 26 is given its rightful place as a watershed moment in the movement of the overall story.

- The tone of the text is consistent with dividing at chapter 26. Prior to this point, the text is rather bleak about the state of the nation. Afterwards there is much more optimism about inheriting the land.

- This structure sits comfortably with the narrative progression of the text. We could repeat our graph, adding a few captions.

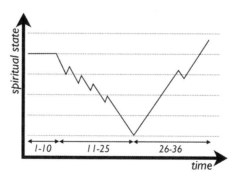

- As we shall see in just a moment, this structure is also sympathetic to the way that both Old and New Testament writers understand the meaning of the book.

- It also reflects the change in leadership which the text reinforces. Chapters 1–25 describe the era of Moses and Aaron whilst the second section carefully explains that Joshua and Eleazar are now the leaders.

- Most importantly, however, this *spiritual* structure allows us to anchor our understanding of any particular passage in the general sense of the book. In the first section, there is warning – an example to avoid. In the second, there is encouragement, an example to emulate.

On this basis, the book has two clear sections:

- Part 1: 'Death in the wilderness'. *The old generation rebels and dies* (Num. 1–25)

- Part 2: 'Life in the promised land'. *The new generation obeys and lives* (Num. 26–36)

For sure, there are ups amongst the downs of the first section: for example, the successful battle of Arad (21:1-3). There is also, possibly, a down amongst the ups of part 2 (chapter 32, though this only applies to two tribes – Gad and Reuben). Also, part 1 could be further subdivided as the first 10 chapters describe good times for Israel. Though they have not yet set out on their journey, they seem to be obedient and faithful. I have represented this on the graph as something of a plateau, though it must be remembered that the post-escape chapters of Exodus hardly paint this generation in a positive light.

So, perhaps we could expand the outline a little:

- Part 1: Death in the wilderness
  - *A good beginning (1–10)*
  - *An inevitable end (11–25)*

- Part 2: Life in the promised land
  - *A new generation (26–36)*

What's the story behind Numbers?

It is important for us to set the biblical context for the book of Numbers. The Pentateuch tells the unfolding story of how the promises made to Abraham are being fulfilled. Numbers plays an important part in this unpacking – for it focuses in particular on two of the three promises made to Abram in Genesis 12 (people, land and blessing). Whilst it is not immediately clear how the people of Numbers will be a blessing to others (at this stage they are mostly *fighting* enemies, not *blessing* them), the fulfilment of the promises regarding the number of Abram's descendants (as numerous as stars in the sky – see Genesis 15:5) and the land (Gen. 12:1) is clear.

The New Testament makes it clear that these promises are fulfilled in Christ, the seed of Abraham (see, for example, Gal. 3:16). Indeed, 'Abraham and his offspring received the promise that he would be heir of the *world* (Rom. 4:13, my italics). The physical realities of Abrahamic fulfilment seen in Numbers point towards greater and eternal spiritual realities in Christ, 'guaranteed to all Abraham's offspring…to all those who are of the faith of Abraham' (Rom. 4:16).

These are important truths to keep in mind whilst reading or studying Numbers. Whilst Christians may hold different views about the ongoing nature of Israel and the place of the physical land in God's purposes, it is clear that the ultimate realities to which Numbers points are the spiritual and faith-led fulfilment of promises made to Abram and found only in Christ.

WHO WROTE NUMBERS DOWN?

We need only say a little about authorship. Traditionally these first five books of the Bible are known as the books of Moses, though the only clue we get that Moses is the original author of Numbers is found in 33:2. Some commentators argue that Moses cannot be the author for it is clearly self-contradictory for the most humble of men to write 'Moses was a very humble man, more humble than anyone else on the face of the earth' (12:3)! However, the traditional arguments for Moses being the author are almost certainly right.

To be exact, precise human authorship is never clarified in the text but, as Christians who have read the rest of the Bible, we are confident that the Holy Spirit 'breathed out' the book. Thus, though certain hard sections may seem out of place (conveniently for some readers who simply wish them away) we should always be thinking 'why is this here, at this place? The Holy Spirit has inspired it for a reason.'

REBELLIONS, REBELLIONS, REBELLIONS

It is worth mentioning that a key feature of the central section of the book (chs. 11 to 25) is one of rebellion. Chapter 11 opens with a very brief, general but typical account. The people grumble, the Lord responds in judgment, the people cry out to Moses, who intercedes for them and the Lord's anger diminishes. Nearly all the rebellions that follow take the same pattern.

There are, depending on the method of counting, about 13 of these rebellions. Subsequent rebellions do not necessarily add new information all the time, other than reinforcing that the grumbling spirit of this first generation is never really changed. Even after the ultimate judgment (death in the wilderness, chs. 13 and 14), this complaining continues. Everyone is affected. Only Joshua and Caleb from the first generation ever enter the land.

Although it is difficult to convey in a little book like this, the repetition of the rebellions itself serves a purpose. I remember watching a highly effective TV war series (*Band of Brothers*) where the bombing of the front line continued throughout the particular episode. After a while, it simply became numbing: 'surely that must be the end?' I thought to myself. But it continued. This same effective technique is being used here to make a point about the hearts of the Israelites. The fact that the rebellions keep coming and coming makes the reader feel quite numb. Though you may be tempted to skip over some of these passages, to do so would be to lose the purpose of the text in painting a bleak picture of the state of a rebellious heart, unchanged by a seemingly never-ending cycle of complaint-repentance-complaint.

The table below gives some idea of these rebellions. The key one is that of the entire people (save Joshua and Caleb) against Yahweh regarding the occupation of the land (chapter 14, highlighted in the table). This is the well-known story of the spies and the primary cause of the generation dying in the wilderness.

Rebellion	Reference	Place
Assembly and hardships	11:1-3	Taberah
Assembly and the manna	11:4-34	Kibroth Hattaavah
Moses against Yahweh	11:18-21	Kibroth Hattaavah
Miriam/Aaron against Moses	12:1-2	Hazeroth
10 spies	13:31	Paran
Assembly and the conquest	14:1-4	Kadesh in Paran
Assembly and presumption	14:44	'High hill country'
Korah/Dathan/Abiram/250 leaders	16:1-3	
Assembly against Moses	16:41	
Assembly and the water	20:1-13	Kadesh in Zin
Assembly against Moses	21:4	Around Edom
Seduced by Moabites	25:1-18	Shittim
Gad & Reuben reject promised land	32	Plains of Moab

2

Why should I read Numbers?

Why should a twenty-first-century reader bother with Numbers? At one level, there's a very easy answer. It's in our Bibles and we firmly believe, therefore, that it was breathed out by God and useful for 'teaching, rebuking, correcting and training in righteousness' (2 Tim. 3:16). But, more precisely, there are two main reasons for Christians to read and rejoice in the Bible book of Numbers, both of which we get from the Bible itself.

NUMBERS PROCLAIMS CHRIST

The first is that, like all of Scripture, Numbers proclaims Christ. Our biblical theology teaches us that, in the words of one of my daughter's Bibles, 'every story whispers his name.'[1] Jesus teaches the pair on the road to Emmaus: 'and beginning with Moses and all the Prophets, he explained to them what was said in all the Scriptures concerning himself' (Luke 24:27). 'Moses' here represents the books of Moses – the first five books of the Bible. In what way, however, does Numbers speak of Christ?

First, it speaks of Him *indirectly*. The whole of the Old Testament fits together to anticipate the coming of the Saviour of the world. As such, any Old Testament passage is part of a trajectory which takes us, ultimately, to the incarnation, life, death

---

1   Sally Lloyd-Jones, *The Jesus Storybook Bible* (Grand Rapids, USA: Zondervan, 2007)

and resurrection of Christ (and beyond, of course). In this sense we should expect to see urgent anticipation of the Messiah.

Such anticipation is sometimes seen *negatively* in terms of how desperate the state of the people is without the lasting forgiveness and life-changing power that the coming of Christ brings. Along the way in Numbers, we shall find plenty of allusions and hints that make us cry out 'How long, O Lord?' But it is also seen *positively*, especially in those who foreshadow Christ. Moses, in particular, is singled out in both the Old Testament and New as someone special — there is *no-one* like Moses (12:3 and Heb. 3:2-3). The various administrations of the covenant (especially the sacrifices) also look forward to Christ, the once-for-all sacrifice for sins.

There are also more *direct* proclamations of Christ. Sometimes these

references are obscure without the il-
lumination of the New Testament. Two
examples will suffice:

- The Apostle John identifies the bronze
  snake (Num. 21:9 – an incident which
  plays only a small part in the overall
  story) as being a foreshadowing of
  the lifting up of the Christ upon the
  cross (John 3:14–15).

- The Apostle Paul identifies the
  water-providing rock (Num. 20)
  as Christ Himself, from whom the
  Israelites could drink both physically
  and spiritually (1 Cor. 10:4)

Of course, you need good Bible knowledge
to be able to spot these! But a good cross-
reference Bible or a simple commentary like
those I've listed at the end of this book will
help enormously. We must let Scripture
interpret Scripture and ensure that the link
to Christ is made in our reading.

There is a danger, however, in seeing such indirect allusions under every rock (literally!). Some older commentaries, in particular, saw such allusions in all sorts of wonderful places. Better, I think, to make the connections where Scripture does and let the Scriptures be the best interpreter of themselves.

However, there are more direct prophecies as well. Christ is supremely Israel, God's firstborn and beloved Son. He thus fulfils the glorious expectations that are placed upon Him in Balaam's prophecies. Here is highly exalted language fit for a king: 'I see him, but not now; I behold him, but not near. A star will come out of Jacob; a sceptre will rise out of Israel' (Num. 24:17).

Remember, we're not just reading Numbers as a Jewish book, even though it was that originally. This is Christian Scripture, and as such its aim and purpose is to proclaim 'Jesus Christ and him crucified' (1 Cor. 2:2).

NUMBERS GIVES US AN EXAMPLE TO AVOID (OR FOLLOW)

The temptation is to think that seeing Christ in the sweep of the historical context of the Old Testament stops us from drawing any ethical or moral application. However, that's simply not true. Both Old and New Testament writers certainly saw no embarrassment in understanding Numbers this way. It is worth a quick survey of the four key passages which comment on Numbers.

Psalm 95

Psalm 95 is a brief psalm which calls on God's people to sing and shout aloud to the 'Rock of our salvation'. He is the one who is a great King, the creator and sustainer of the planet, our shepherd (vv. 1-7). The application that flows from these great truths is that we should not harden our hearts towards Him.

This, says the psalmist, is what happened at Meribah and Massah 'in the desert' (v. 8). These two places relate the psalm back to the account of grumbling found in Exodus 17 (Exod. 17:7). Massah means 'testing' and Meribah means 'quarrelling'. (Interestingly, Meribah is also the name given to a place in Numbers where a similar incident occurs – see Numbers 20:13.)

However, the psalmist seems to be thinking about the whole journey from Egypt to Canaan – not just the Exodus account – for he repeats God's condemnation, 'for forty years I was angry with that generation...' (v. 10), which itself relates not to grumbling over water but a refusal to go into the land, an incident which takes place in Numbers (Num. 14).

Therefore, the psalmist applies a broad lesson to the wandering years which is essentially this: 'don't make the same mistake they did.'

Hebrews 3–4

This same passage and application is picked up in Hebrews 3–4, particularly 3:7–4:13. There we have a Bible study (the Hebrews passage) on a Bible study (Ps. 95), with an extensive analysis of the psalm. The passage is far from straight-forward, tackling as it does the biblical theology of rest and Sabbath. In the Old Testament, 'rest' is sometimes a synonym for the promised land.

The writer argues that the warning of Psalm 95 'Do not harden your hearts' still stands today because the threat 'they shall never enter my rest' also still stands. How so? Surely when the people conquered Canaan they entered the rest? Not so, argues the writer. For then, Psalm 95 (written as it was after the conquest) could not have said 'Today'. 'Rest' must mean more than the promised land. Indeed, it means, ultimately, the Sabbath-rest that

God already enjoys – nothing less than eternal peace and presence with Him.

That is why the promise still stands (as does the warning). This elevates Numbers and its story of being careful not to fall in the desert to the highest level. On this understanding, Numbers is a picture of our own wilderness wanderings and we must be careful to enter into our own promised land, our own 'rest' – the 'Sabbath-rest for the people of God' (Heb. 4:9).

An interesting aside is that the most famous part of this Hebrews passage is set in its proper context. 'For the word of God is living and active. Sharper than any double-edged sword, it penetrates even to dividing soul and spirit, joints and marrow; it judges the thoughts and attitudes of the heart. Nothing in all creation is hidden from God's sight. Everything is uncovered and laid bare before the eyes of Him to whom we must give account.' (Heb. 4:12-13). This text is often used as a comfort, but in the context of Hebrews 3 and 4 and the setting of Numbers it is actually about judgment. The Word of God comes as a word of wrath in Numbers to prevent the people from entering the promised land. Hardly warming in the way we normally present it!

In fact, the whole book of Hebrews appears to be a commentary on the book of Numbers. Not only are there direct references like those above, but the book is full of allusions to Numbers material. Reading Numbers alongside Hebrews is a remarkably rewarding exercise. Why not give it a go?

Psalm 106
Psalm 106 is a long psalm beginning with the common refrain 'Praise the Lord.' It describes the history of the nation from Egypt to Ezekiel. However, the bulk of the text focuses on the events of Numbers. Verse 13 begins the Numbers story (though it does scoot back to Exodus every now and

again). Many of the individual narratives warrant particular attention: the failure to listen to Joshua and Caleb (Num. 13, Ps. 106:24-27); the monumental failure at Shittim (Num. 25, Ps. 106:28-31); even Moses' failure to honour the Lord as holy (Num. 20, Ps. 106:32-33). The events of Numbers are not recounted in the psalm in strict chronological order. Nonetheless, it is clear that something is to be gained from a review of the nation's history.

What is it? It is:

- a call to praise the faithful Lord who brought them through it: 'Give thanks to the Lord, for he is good, his love endures for ever' (v. 1) and 'Praise be to the LORD, the God of Israel, from everlasting to everlasting. Let all the people say, "Amen!" Praise the LORD.' (v. 48)

- a plea to God to go on saving them. 'Save us, O LORD our God, and gather us from the nations, that we may give thanks to your holy name and glory in your praise.' (v. 47)

In other words, the psalmist recognizes that the intrinsic nature of the people's failure in the desert remains. At the time of writing the psalm – many years after the Numbers story – the people of God *still* need God to save them: that is their only hope.

There is a good symmetry here with the Pentateuch. Some commentators think that the five books of Psalms mirror to some extent the first five books of The Law; if this is, so then this, the last psalm of Book IV, ought in some way to expound on the fourth book of the Pentateuch, which just happens to be Numbers!

1 Corinthians 10:1-14

Psalm 106 is more detailed than Psalm 95 in its analysis of the wilderness wanderings and, similarly, 1 Corinthians 10 examines the accounts in more detail than Hebrews 3–4.

Again, there is clear reference to some of the post-Exodus stories. Verse 7 of 1 Corinthians 10 refers to the incident of the Golden Calf in Exodus 32. However, the remaining references are almost certainly all to Numbers: verse 8 refers to Numbers 25; verse 9 refers to Numbers 21; and verse 10, though slightly obscure, probably refers to Numbers 11.

Paul is unashamed to spiritualize the journey and draw moral lessons from it. For the physical realities had real spiritual meaning – 'they were all baptized into Moses in the cloud and in the sea. They all ate the same spiritual food and drank the same spiritual drink; for they drank from the spiritual rock that accompanied them, and that rock was Christ' (vv. 2-4).

This last statement is perhaps the most surprising. The rock, the miraculous source of their refreshment was itself an allusion to Christ. Paul thus makes the stories of Numbers highly relevant to Christians today: 'these things occurred as examples to keep us from setting our hearts on evil things as they did' (v. 6). So, his primary application from reading Numbers is that Christians today should not be 'idolaters' nor 'commit sexual immorality' nor 'test the Lord' nor 'grumble'.

In fact, if we think we are so secure, we'd better take care! 'Be careful that you don't fall!' (v. 12). However, for our encouragement we also learn that 'No temptation has seized you except what is common to man. And God is faithful; he will not let you be tempted beyond what you can bear. But when you are tempted, he will also provide a way out so that you can stand up under it' (v. 13) – a lesson that the wilderness generation failed to learn or apply.

We can certainly read Numbers with this ethical outlook; indeed it would be wrong not to. But how does it fit with what people sometimes call the biblical theology, that is, that all of Scripture points and takes us to Christ. 1 Corinthians perhaps provides the answer. The two are not inconsistent for all, along, Christ journeyed with them. They were not alone and their moral failure was actually their failure to see Christ amongst them and fix themselves upon Him.

Seeing Christ in all the Scriptures and understanding our call to moral obedience before a holy God are therefore not mutually exclusive. Rather, they are gloriously one and the same thing. We could say, therefore, that Numbers gives us an example to follow as it proclaims Christ in all His glory and goodness.

I take it that we can also apply this approach *positively*. Although both 1 Corinthians and Hebrews do so *negatively* ('Don't be like them'), we can infer that where Numbers is positive, we can be too. Take the daughters of Zelophehad (chs. 27 and 36). These five women walk by faith and believe in the inheritance. They are willing to do whatever is needed to claim and keep the inheritance allotted to them. They do not fall in the wilderness but, rather, are heroines of the faith. We are not to be like their father Zelophehad who did fall in the desert. But we can apply the same New Testament principle to say that we should marvel and imitate the attitude and faith of his five girls.

Let's now take a closer look at the most important of these passages for our reading of Numbers: Paul's words to the Christians at Corinth.

HISTORY DOESN'T REPEAT ITSELF, BUT IT DOES RHYME

Mark Twain, that clever wit, was reputed to have said, 'History doesn't repeat itself, but it does rhyme.' Sadly, there is no record of him ever saying such a thing! But the point is a good one. Things that happen in the past never quite come around the same again. Not exactly. But the same *kinds* of things do repeat. And Christians should not be surprised at that for we know that hearts do not change, God does not change and, therefore, the problems and joys of life that arise keep on arising. It is always wise to learn from the past, and the Apostle Paul tells us that it is no different for Christians.

Take a closer look at 1 Corinthians 10:1-14.

> For I do not want you to be ignorant of the fact, brothers, that our forefathers were all under the cloud and that they all passed through the sea. [2] They were all baptised into Moses in the cloud and in the sea. [3] They all ate the same spiritual food [4] and drank the same spiritual drink; for they drank from the spiritual rock that accompanied them, and that rock was Christ. [5]Nevertheless, God was not pleased with most of them; their bodies were scattered over the desert.

⁶Now these things occurred as examples to keep us from setting our hearts on evil things as they did. ⁷Do not be idolaters, as some of them were; as it is written: 'The people sat down to eat and drink and got up to indulge in pagan revelry.' ⁸We should not commit sexual immorality, as some of them did— and in one day twenty-three thousand of them died. ⁹We should not test the Lord, as some of them did—and were killed by snakes. ¹⁰And do not grumble, as some of them did—and were killed by the destroying angel.

¹¹These things happened to them as examples and were written down as warnings for us, on whom the fulfil-ment of the ages has come. ¹²So, if you think you are standing firm, be careful that you don't fall! ¹³No temptation has seized you except what is common to man. And God is faithful; he will not let you be tempted beyond what you can bear. But when you are tempted, he will

also provide a way out so that you can stand up under it.

¹⁴Therefore, my dear friends, flee from idolatry.

Here, the Apostle draws parallels between the people of Numbers and the Corinthians to whom he writes. His references to 'eating' and 'drinking' (v. 3) are almost certainly a reference to the Lord's Supper – the subject of this section of the epistle. But the point is clear – there is a connection between the historical people and God's people today. 'These things occurred as examples to keep us from setting our hearts on evil things as they did' (v. 6). The lessons are clear and explained one by one in the text:

- Do not be idolaters (v. 7)

- Do not commit sexual immorality (v. 8)

- Do not test the Lord (v. 9)

- Do not grumble (v. 10)

Each of these headings refers back to biblical stories in Numbers (in three of the cases) and Exodus (in the other). They convey a broadly negative lesson: do not make the same mistakes that the people of God made back then. But there is more for us here than warning. For sure, we need to be careful that we don't fall. However, there is also exhortation for us.

The point of the passage is that we do not need to make the same mistakes that the wanderers did. When we are tempted 'he will also provide a way out so that you can stand up under it' (v. 13). 'Therefore, my dear friends, flee from idolatry' (v. 14).

In fact, even more incredibly, the wilderness people had this same promise for the rock that accompanied them was Christ (v. 4). Christ Jesus is eternally the

Son of God, and though He took on flesh in one moment in history, before that He was with His people just as He is today. In reading Numbers, we must never say that they were different from us and so failure was inevitable. No! They had Christ with them, just as we do today.

Here are some questions which will help you think about this passage more deeply and so be prepared to get into reading the book of Numbers. They are all based on the 1 Corinthians 10 passage.

Questions to help understand the passage

1. What is the context of this warning to the Corinthians? See 1 Corinthians 8 and 1 Corinthians 10:14-22.

2. What links or similarities are there between the people who wandered in the desert and the Corinthian Christians (vv. 1-5)?

3. What surprises you about what Paul says? How does that help us understand Numbers better?

4. What is the main lesson to be learnt (v. 6)?

5. What four sub-lessons does this break down into (vv. 7-10)?

6. Try to see if you can link these lessons to specific incidents in Exodus or Numbers. Use a cross-reference Bible to help you.

7. What warnings are contained in verses 12-14?

8. What encouragements are contained in verses 12-14?

Questions to help apply the passage

1. How does this passage help us read the stories in Numbers?

2. The examples Paul quotes all seem quite extreme. How can we apply them to our lives?

3. How does having Christ with us on our journey make a difference to how we live?

4. What does verse 13 mean in practice? How can we use it positively to avoid the mistakes of the wilderness generation?

HELP FOR READING NUMBERS

There is no doubt that reading Numbers presents some particular challenges for a reader, even a confident one! Here are some practical ideas for reading Numbers through.

1. Read the book using a translation you feel comfortable with. There are good English translations of every level. Use one where you feel happy with the language and vocabulary. Trying

to read Numbers with a Bible where there are lots of words you don't understand will be very difficult. Just check that the version you use doesn't miss out any parts of Numbers. The simplest way to do this is to go to chapter 7 and make sure all the verses are there!

2. Read in fairly large chunks. If you start a story make sure you read it through to the end. You could use my reading plan (see below) which breaks down Numbers into 17 manageable sections but keeps closely related stories together.

3. Think about investing in a simple commentary. The list at the end has one or two ideas. The study notes in the esv Study Bible are also an excellent help.

4. Keep asking yourself how the text points to Jesus and tells us what it means to follow Him. To be honest, in some passages that is sometimes more difficult than in others: this is where a simple commentary may help.

5. Don't ask questions of the text it doesn't seek to answer. People often question, for example, whether the generation who died in the wilderness were true believers. The answer is that some of them certainly were (for example, Moses) and some of them certainly were not (for example, Korah). But the Bible text never really seeks to answer that question, and so we should probably avoid asking it!

6. Don't be afraid of lists. They are inspired too and often the way that they are written makes a point in itself. For example, the repetition of Numbers 7 makes a very strong point about the

unity of the tribes which is lost if the rhythm and cadence of the repetition is missing.

7. Think of the violence in Numbers as righteous judgment rather than violence for its own sake. Rebellious people who have turned their back on God do not deserve His grace. And so individuals, families and nations who do this suffer the consequences of their rebellion. In fact, it is good to remember that the most astounding fact about Numbers is that *more* people are not judged and killed. God is gracious. And remember that sometimes Israel herself is judged, and sometimes she is the instrument of God's judgment against others.

Here is a plan you might like to use. It will help you read through Numbers in 17 days.

Above all, I hope and pray that this is a book you will find enjoyable and rewarding as it teaches you more about the Lord Jesus Christ and what it means to follow Him.

Further reading

There are a number of excellent commentaries on Numbers. I have listed some simple ones that would help the ordinary Bible reader. I think that Martin Pakula's is the best of this group.

Raymond Brown, *The Bible Speaks Today, Numbers* (Nottingham, U.K.: IVP, 2002)

Iain M. Duguid, *Numbers: God's presence in the wilderness* (Wheaton, U.S.A.: Crossway, 2006)

Martin Pakula, *Homeward Bound: Reading Numbers Today* (Sydney, Australia: Aquila Press, 2006)

In addition, if you have any teaching responsibility in the church (for example, leading a small group) or even if you want to think through the meaning and application for each day's reading in my list above, please do think about getting the full volume of *Teaching Numbers*, of which this is a small taster.

Also available in this series ...

Introducing Series

Introducing 1 Timothy
(ANGUS MACLEAY)

Introducing Acts
(DAVID COOK)

Introducing Ephesians
(SIMON AUSTEN)

Introducing Numbers
(ADRIAN REYNOLDS)

Introducing Romans
(CHRISTOPHER ASH)

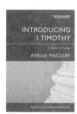

978-1-78191-060-3

978-1-84550-824-1

978-1-78191-059-7

978-1-78191-158-7

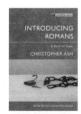

978-1-78191-233-1

These are books which will equip you for your own study of Ephesians, 1 Timothy, Acts, Numbers, Daniel and Romans, ultimately in teaching them. It will help you answer the questions: Why did things happen the way they did? Why should we read these books of the Bible today? What are the main themes? These are Pocket Guide versions of *Teaching 1 Timothy* (978-1-84550-808-1), *Teaching Acts* (978-1-84550-255-3), *Teaching Ephesians* (978-1-84550-684-1), *Teaching Numbers* (978-1-78191-156-3), *Teaching Romans vol. 1* (978-1-84550-455-7) and *Teaching Romans vol. 2* (978-1-84550-456-4). Each includes an introductory study.

Christopher Ash is Director of the Cornhill Training Course, a one-year course designed to provide Bible-handling and practical ministry skills to those exploring their future role in Christian work, and an active member of Christ Church Mayfair in central London.

Simon Austen has degrees in Science and Theology. A previous chaplain of Stowe School in Buckinghamshire, he is now Vicar of Houghton and Kingmoor in Carlisle, England.

David Cook has recently retired from his role as Principal and Director of the School of Preaching at Sydney Missionary and Bible College (SMBC). He is now involved in an itinerant preaching and teaching ministry.

Angus MacLeay is the Rector of St Nicholas, a large Anglican church in Sevenoaks, Kent, and is also a member of the Church of England General Synod.

Adrian Reynolds is Director of Ministry of The Proclamation Trust and also serves as associate minister at East London Tabernacle Baptist Church.

PT Resources

www.proctrust.org.uk
Resources for preachers and Bible teachers

PT Resources, a ministry of The Proclamation Trust, provides a range of multimedia resources for preachers and Bible teachers.

Books

The *Teaching the Bible* series, published jointly with *Christian Focus Publications*, is written by preachers, for preachers, and is specifically geared to the purpose of God's Word – its proclamation as living truth. Books in the series aim to help the reader move beyond simply understanding a text to communicating and applying it.

Current titles include: *Teaching 1 Peter, Teaching 1 Timothy, Teaching Acts, Teaching Amos, Teaching Ephesians, Teaching Isaiah, Teaching Matthew, Teaching Numbers, Teaching Romans,* and *Teaching the Christian Hope.*

Forthcoming titles include: *Teaching Daniel*, *Teaching 1 and 2 Kings*, and *Teaching Nehemiah*.

DVD TRAINING

Preaching & Teaching the Old Testament:
4 DVDs – Narrative, Prophecy, Poetry, Wisdom

Preaching & Teaching the New Testament
3 DVDs – Gospels, Letters, Acts & Revelation

These training DVDs aim to give preachers and teachers confidence in handling the rich variety of God's Word. David Jackman has taught this material to generations of Cornhill students, and gives us step-by-step instructions on handling each genre of biblical literature.

He demonstrates principles that will guide us through the challenges of teaching and applying different parts of the Bible, for example:

- How does prophecy relate to the lives of its hearers – ancient and modern?
- How can you preach in a way that reflects the deep emotion of the Psalms?

Both sets are suitable for preachers and for those teaching the Bible in a wide variety of contexts.

- Designed for **individual** and **group** study
- Interactive learning through many **worked examples** and **exercises**
- Flexible format ideal for **training courses**
- Optional **English subtitles** for second-language users
- Print as many **workbooks** as you need (PDF)

AUDIO
PT Resources has a large range of Mp3 downloads, nearly all of which are entirely free to download and use.

PREACHING INSTRUCTION
This series aims to help the preacher or teacher understand, open up and teach individual books of the Bible by getting to grips with their central message and purpose.

SERMON SERIES
These sermons, examples of great preaching, not only demonstrate faithful biblical preaching but will also refresh and instruct the hearer.

CONFERENCES
Recordings of our conferences include challenging topical addresses, discussion of preaching and ministry issues, and warm-hearted exposition that will challenge and inspire all those in ministry.

Christian Focus Publications

Our mission statement –

STAYING FAITHFUL

In dependence upon God we seek to impact the world through literature faithful to His infallible Word, the Bible. Our aim is to ensure that the Lord Jesus Christ is presented as the only hope to obtain forgiveness of sin, live a useful life and look forward to heaven with Him.

Our books are published in four imprints:

CHRISTIAN FOCUS

popular works including biographies, commentaries, basic doctrine and Christian living.

CHRISTIAN HERITAGE

books representing some of the best material from the rich heritage of the church.

MENTOR

books written at a level suitable for Bible College and seminary students, pastors, and other serious readers. The imprint includes commentaries, doctrinal studies, examination of current issues and church history.

CF4•K

children's books for quality Bible teaching and for all age groups: Sunday school curriculum, puzzle and activity books; personal and family devotional titles, biographies and inspirational stories – Because you are never too young to know Jesus!

Christian Focus Publications Ltd,
Geanies House, Fearn, Ross-shire,
IV20 1TW, Scotland, United Kingdom.
www.christianfocus.com